Michael F. Howley

An Explanation of the Holy Sacrifice of the Mass

Michael F. Howley

An Explanation of the Holy Sacrifice of the Mass

ISBN/EAN: 9783337300487

Printed in Europe, USA, Canada, Australia, Japan

Cover: Foto ©Lupo / pixelio.de

More available books at **www.hansebooks.com**

AN

EXPLANATION

OF THE

Holy Sacrifice of the Mass

EDITED AND REVISED BY THE

RT. REV. M. F. HOWLEY, D.D.
Bishop of West Newfoundland

BOSTON
DOYLE AND WHITTLE
1894

Perlexi libellum cui titulus: "AN EXPLANATION OF THE HOLY SACRIFICE OF THE MASS;" immunem inveni erroribus doctrinalibus, perutilem recussionem censeo.

✠ M. F. HOWLEY,
Vic. Apost.

Imprimatur.
✠ JOANNES JOSEPHUS,
Archiepiscopus Bostoniensis.

BOSTONIÆ, 20ᵃ Apr., 1894.

INTRODUCTION.

THIS unpretentious little volume is republished from an old print, and has been carefully revised and much improved by Right Rev. Bishop HOWLEY. It was intended primarily for the instruction and edification of Catholics, that by a better understanding of the great central act of divine worship, the Holy Sacrifice of the Mass, they may reap therefrom richer profit to their souls.

At the same time, these explanations may serve to satisfy the curiosity, more or less reverent, of non-Catholics who may sometimes witness the solemn, but to them mysterious, services in a Catholic church. Seldom do we find amongst our Protestant friends one who knows anything about our holy religion, its teaching and its practices, except the absurdities which from childhood he has been taught to believe concerning it. It is not uncommon to meet those who have never read a Catholic book or ever entered a Catholic church. Some may not care to hear the truth if it contradicts their deeply-rooted prejudices, and many are, alas! utterly indifferent to the higher life,—to the relations of the soul with God; but there must be some honest minds ready to follow where the kindly light of truth may lead them. If the providence of God should put this little book into the hands of any such truth-loving non-Catholics, we hope it may show them the reasonableness and the sublime significance of those solemn ceremonies and beautiful prayers which to the unfriendly or unsympathetic eye may seem like "empty forms," but which we Catholics intend for the expression of our most reverent and loving worship of the God-Man, Jesus Christ, whom we see with the eyes of faith really and truly present on our altars, where He offers Himself to His Heavenly Father, renewing daily the awful Sacrifice of Calvary.

It is not within the scope of this modest little

book to prove at length the Real Presence and the reality of the Sacrifice of the Mass as the continuation of the Sacrifice of the Cross; but, taking that for granted, as believed by Catholics, the purpose is to show the reason and the meaning of the solemnity with which the Church reverently surrounds that Real Presence and true Sacrifice.

May these pages lead some soul to the better knowledge and greater love of Jesus Christ, the Son of God and Son of Mary, true God and true Man, who died on the Cross for our sins, and who continues to immolate Himself on our altars and dwell in His Real Presence in our tabernacles.

CONTENTS.

CHAPTER	PAGE
I. — DEFINITION OF THE HOLY SACRIFICE OF THE MASS	1
MASS IN LATIN, OBJECTIONS TO	7
II. — DERIVATION AND OFFICE OF THE PRIEST	14
VESTMENTS EXPLAINED:	
THE AMICE	15
ALB	15
GIRDLE	16
MANIPLE	17
STOLE	18
CHAUSABLE	19
ALTAR	20
CRUCIFIX AND CANDLES	21
BEGINNING OF THE MASS	24
CONFITEOR	25
RELICS	27
III. — THE INTROÏT	30
GLORIA	31
DOMINUS VOBISCUM	32
COLLECTS	33
EPISTLE	33
GRADUAL	35

(v)

CONTENTS.

Chapter	Page
III. — THE GOSPEL	35
CREED	37
OFFERTORY	38
ORATE FRATRES	41
SECRET PRAYER	42
PREFACE	43
IV. — THE CANON OF THE MASS	45
PRAYERS FOR THE CHURCH	46
PRAYERS FOR THE CHIEF BISHOP	46
MEMENTO FOR THE LIVING	47
COMMUNICANTES	48
CONSECRATION	53
ENDS OF THE SACRIFICE	56
MEMENTO FOR THE FAITHFUL DEPARTED,	57
V. — THE OUR FATHER	61
PAX DOMINI	65
AGNUS DEI	66
PRAYERS BEFORE RECEIVING	67
COMMUNION IN ONE KIND	68
FORM OF A SPIRITUAL COMMUNION	76
PRAYERS AT THE ABLUTION	80
INSTRUCTIONS BEFORE BAPTISM	83
INSTRUCTIONS BEFORE CHURCHING WOMEN	87
INSTRUCTIONS BEFORE MATRIMONY	89
RULES FOR ATTENDING AT MASS	91
MANNER OF ATTENDING AT VESPERS	95

AN EXPLANATION

OF THE

HOLY SACRIFICE OF THE MASS.

CHAPTER I.

SACRIFICE, in general, may be defined, "An oblation of a material thing made to God by a lawful minister, with a real change, to testify God's supreme dominion and our subjection to him."

That such worship was paid to Almighty God from the beginning of the world, under the law of nature in different nations, in the patriarchal ages, from Abel the Just down to the time of the Mosaic law,—no man, the least versant in ancient history, and especially no Christian who admits of the authenticity of the books of the Old Testament, will or can deny.

That sacrifices of various kinds, agreeing with the above definition, were expressly commanded by Almighty God Himself to the Jewish people, together with ceremonies attending them, is evident from the whole book of Leviticus, and, indeed, from the general tenor of the Old Testament.

It is acknowledged that those sacrifices had no value in themselves; but only in relation to the Sacrifice of the Cross, which was to be accomplished by the Son of God, the Redeemer of the World, the Great Mediator between God and man, and the only Reconciler of God with man. It was from His sacrifice, solely, the foregoing sacrifices drew their power and efficacy.

It is confessed, also, that those Jewish sacrifices were only temporary; but, that sacrifice was not to be laid aside, the prophets bear witness.[1] "I have no pleasure in you, saith the Lord of Hosts. I will not receive a gift of your hand: but, from the rising of the sun, even to the going down, my name is great among the Gentiles, and in every place there

---

[1] Malachi, 1. ver. 10, 11.

is Sacrifice, and there is offered to my name a clean oblation; for my name is great among the Gentiles, saith the Lord of Hosts."

Our Saviour, according to the prophecy of David,[1] was chosen and ordained a Priest by His heavenly Father. "The Lord hath sworn, and will not repent; thou art a priest forever, according to the order of Melchisedec." St. Paul cites this passage, and proves from it the necessity of a new and more perfect priesthood[2] in the new law, according to the order of Melchisedec. Our Saviour never assumed that character, nor officiated in that order (during His mortal life) but at His Last Supper.[3] Then He offered His body and blood[4] under the species of bread and wine;[5] and what He did, He gave power to His apostles to do,[6] and commanded them and their successors to do the same, in commemoration of, and to show forth, His death until His second coming. This is what is performed in the holy sacrifice of the Mass, which may be defined, "The sacrifice of the Evangelical law, instituted by Christ at his Last Supper, consisting of an oblation

---

[1] Ps. clx. 4.   [2] Heb. 5.   [3] St. Matt. xxvi. 26.
[4] St. Mark, xiv. 22.   [5] St. Luke, xxii. 19.   [6] I Cor. xi. 24.

of Christ's body and blood, under the species of bread and wine, for a perpetual memorial of his passion."

It is an oblation of something sensible or external, by which it is distinguished from the internal oblation of our souls and affections. Man consists of soul and body: by the former he must worship God internally in spirit and truth; by the latter, exteriorly and sensibly. "By the heart we believe unto justice; by the mouth confession is made unto salvation."[1] It is offered to God, to whom alone sacrifice, as a testimony of sovereignty, can be offered;[2] and only by ministers, "called by God as Aaron was," that is, lawfully ordained in the succession of the sacred hierarchy. A change is wrought, by the almighty power of God, when the awful words of consecration are pronounced; and all the four great ends of sacrifice are comprehended therein.

This sacrifice is called, by the Greeks, Liturgy; in the Latin Church it has generally received the name of Missa or Mass, from very early ages; by Pope Cornelius, in the third century; by Pope Syl-

---

[1] Rom. x. [2] Heb. 5.

vester, in the fourth; by the second Council of Carthage, in the fourth; by the Council of Mileve, 407. It has obtained different names in different places; but the same thing is signified. The Liturgies differ somewhat in words, and in ceremonies, but the substance of all is the same; and the belief of the Real Presence has never varied in the Universal Church spread throughout the world. The Liturgics are yet extant which go under the names of St. Peter, St. James, St. Basil, St. Chrysostom, St. Ambrose, etc. St. Alexander, Pope and martyr, says:[1] " Nothing can be greater in the sacrifice than the body and blood of our Lord Jesus Christ, nor oblation better or more excellent than this, which surpasseth all others."

St. Cyprian observes:[2] "If Jesus Christ, our God and Lord, be the great Priest of God the Father, and hath first offered sacrifice to God, and commanded that we should do this in commemoration of him, certainly the priest holds truly the place of Jesus Christ who doth that which Christ did, and offers the true and entire sacrifice to God the Father in the Church. Therefore, in

---

[1] Anno 121. Ep. 1.   [2] L. 2. Ep. 3.

all sacrifices, we make commemoration of his passion," etc.

Eusebius, Bishop of Cæsarea, and father of church history, remarks: "We sacrifice to the Most High God the complete, dread, and most holy sacrifice, a pure and clean host, in a manner suitable to the New Testament."

St. Chrysostom says:[1] "The priest at the altar offers thanksgiving to God for the whole world by the intended sacrifice."

St. Ambrose testifies:[2] "It is manifest that oblations of beasts which were in Aaron's order are vanished, but Melchisedec's institution remains, and is celebrated all the world over."

St. Augustine, by way of excellency, names it *the Holy Mass, the sacrifice of the Altar, the holy and mystical sacrifice of the New Testament*, the sacrifice of the Church, etc.

From these authorities it is clear that sacrifice has continued in the new law, and that this sacrifice in the Western Church, from early antiquity, has obtained the name of Mass.

St. Paul reasons with his brethren, the Jews,

---
[1] Homil. 26, in Mat.   [2] In 3 Cap. Heb.

that as perfection was not to be had by the Levitical priesthood, it became necessary that another priesthood should arise according to the order of Melchisedec.[1] And the same apostle beautifully shows Melchisedec, and his sacrifice of bread and wine, to have been an illustrious figure of our Saviour, and His priesthood and sacrifice, and, consequently, of the unbloody sacrifice, which has been, is, and ever will be offered in the Church, as the perpetual commemoration of our Saviour's death; not as supposing any deficiency in the sacrifice of the cross, but as the continuance and daily application of its merits, to procure graces, which, though purchased, were not actually bestowed, and for the forgiveness of sins, which, not being yet committed, could not be then forgiven.

MASS IN LATIN.

One of the most common and specious objections to our Liturgy is, that it is said in the Latin and not in the vulgar tongue. In answer to this, we observe, 1st, That there were three languages, as it were, consecrated by the inscription on our

---

[1] Heb. vii.

Saviour's cross, viz., the Hebrew or Syro-Chaldaic, the Greek, and Latin; in which languages all the Liturgies used in the Primitive Church were written and said: the Hebrew for Palestine and its vicinity, where that language was understood; the Greek for the Oriental countries, and the Latin for the western parts. The vernacular tongues, in all these countries, have since changed and are still changing; but the Liturgies have not changed nor been translated into all the changing dialects, lest they might be thereby corrupted and altered. The Eastern Church, in all its latitude, even amongst people of divers nations, which now all speak other languages, celebrates the Liturgy in pure Greek; and in the Western Church it is, and always was, said in Latin (excepting only a temporary dispensation given to the Sclavonians to facilitate their conversion). In the Apostles' time, the Latin, we may say, was the vulgar tongue of Europe as well as of Africa, and is still the most commonly known by educated persons in every part of Europe. It is not the Church which has introduced a foreign language, but it is the people who have forgotten their ancient tongue. It is natural enough that the

Church of England, which is of modern date, and confined to its own domain, should adopt its own language in its Liturgy.[1] As to the Church of Scotland, having no Liturgy, it has been saved the trouble of translating, modelling, and remodelling like that of England; but the Catholic Church, claiming greater antiquity, and greater extent, retains its ancient language, which affords its ministers an opportunity of officiating wheresoever they may be; and the laity, finding the service of the Church the same in all countries, find themselves always at home whithersoever they travel.[2]

The people are not ignorant of what is said. The Mass is translated into the ordinary language of the country for their private satisfaction, and they are furnished with explanations of the different parts; and as the priest and the people act in very different capacities, the laity are accommodated with prayers suited to their state, or, knowing well the several parts of the Sacrifice, they can

---

[1] Dr. Milner.

[2] In Shanghai, China, one has assisted at Mass in a congregation of Chinese, Japanese, Spanish, Malays, Portuguese, French, Germans, Italians, and English. In what church or office except the Catholic Mass could these different nationalities feel at home?

adapt thereto the becoming reverence of their bodies, and the piety and devotion of their minds. Whosoever will take the trouble to observe the decorum, silence, attention, and devotion of a decent Catholic audience during Mass, and compare these with the demeanor of any other body of Christians at any part of their worship, will in all probability divest himself of all or much of his prejudice against the Mass in Latin.

2d. Let it also be observed, that the people do not hear Mass for instruction, but to join with their brethren there present, and with the whole Church, to pay their adoration, praise, and thanksgiving to the Almighty; to commemorate our Saviour's passion and death; and to solicit, through their common Mediator, the graces and blessings He has purchased for them by His sufferings. It is obvious to all, that solid instruction, in the articles of faith, and the sublime morality of the gospel, is afforded to Catholics by sermons and catechisms in the vulgar tongue; besides the pious and forcible lessons and admonitions they receive in the tribunal of penance.

To illustrate this subject still further, it ought to

be recollected, that the temple of Jerusalem was divided into different apartments and enclosures. The high priest alone went into the remotest sanctuary, once a year, to make a solemn atonement.[1] The next enclosure was allotted for the priests only, to offer the usual sacrifices, and renew the loaves of Proposition. If any of the Jewish laity had dared to set a foot therein, the law commanded that he should be stoned as a sacrilegious profaner. Even King Oziah, who thought he might, by the privilege of his royal dignity, enter in thither and offer incense, was instantly covered with leprosy, degraded from royalty, and separated, for the remainder of his days, from the society and intercourse of mankind.[2]

In this enclosure, Zachary, the father of the Baptist, offered incense by himself.[3] The multitude of the people saw the smoke ascending, but they neither saw nor heard the priest; yet they joined in the sacrifice, and were *praying*, meantime, without, in that division where the Israelites were allowed to enter after the necessary purifications, and which was yet separated from the court, where

---

[1] Levit. xvi. [2] II Chron. xxvi. [3] St. Luke i. 10, etc.

strangers and Gentiles were instructed in the law of Moses.

During the Babylonish captivity, the Israelites forgot their language; yet the Scriptures and Jewish Liturgy were read in the temple and synagogues in pure Hebrew, and the priests and doctors of the law explained them, and made homilies and commentaries upon them to the people.

The objection from St. Paul, I Cor. xiv., is nothing to the purpose. The apostle speaks not, there, of the public service, but of private conferences among the laity newly converted, who have often shared in the exterior miraculous gifts of the Holy Ghost, such as prophecy and the gift of tongues; and which were sometimes abused through ostentation, etc. The apostle, in this chapter, wished to correct those abuses and disorders.

Luther himself, against Carlostad, maintained that the language of public worship was a matter of indifference. When Queen Elizabeth wished to convert the Irish to her new faith, she sent to Ireland her supernumerary Levites with her English Liturgy, of which the Irish understood not a word, no more than her clergy understood the Irish language.

How few understand, by the ear, what is sung in any church? and what can the greater part of the people make of the Psalms of David even when translated into the vulgar tongue? The most learned theologians have often great difficulty in ascertaining their literal meaning.

The Catholic Church has succeeded much better in uniting the hearts of the faithful in the same faith, and in agreement of devotion to the same sacrifice, by retaining her ancient language, than kings, queens, and parliaments, by their acts of uniformity and penal statutes.

CHAPTER II.

DERIVATION AND OFFICE OF A PRIEST.

THE word Priest may be derived from Πρεσβυτερος or Πρεσβυτης, which, in the New Testament, always signifies a pastor of the Church. Ιερευς, Sacerdos, Priest, always in the Greek meant a sacrificer, — one who, as a public minister, offers sacrifice. St. Paul gives this definition of a priest: That he is "one taken from among men in the things that appertain to God, that he may offer up gifts and sacrifices for sins."[1]

VESTMENTS EXPLAINED.

When we read in Chapter xxvii. of Exodus the command of Almighty God for the vestments of Aaron and his sons, the magnificence, glory, and beauty of that vesture prescribed by God Himself, in which they were to perform the offices of the priesthood, we need not wonder that the priests of the new law, which is far more holy and sublime,

---
[1] Heb. chap. v. 1.

should, in offering holy sacrifice, have a certain habit to distinguish them from the rest of the faithful, both to put themselves in mind of their awful duty, and to move the people to greater respect and reverence to the sacred mysteries.

AMICE.

The Amice, which signifies Veil, is a piece of linen which the priest puts on his head and lets fall down on his shoulders (hence called also *humerale*), and fastens with strings before him. In allusion to the Christian armor mentioned by St. Paul,[1] he says, in putting it on, "Place on my head, O Lord, the helmet of salvation for the vanquishing the devil's assaults." Mystically, the Amice denotes the Veil which was put on our Saviour's face by the Jews, blindfolding Him, and saying, "Prophecy unto us, O Christ, who it was that struck thee."[2]

THE ALB.

The Alb is a white linen tunic with sleeves, and descending to the feet, whence it is called Ποδήρης,

---

[1] Eph. vi.   [2] Matt. xxvi. 68.

or *vestis talaris*. The whiteness of this and the foregoing vestment signifies the purity necessary for approaching the altar. In the law of Moses, frequent mention is made of linen tunics among the sacerdotal vestments. St. Jerome affirms,[1] that St. James, the Apostle, used linen clothes in celebrating Mass. St. Ambrose, St. Gregory, and Venerable Bede, expressly mention the alb, amice, and stole, used by him, and long after preserved in Jerusalem. St. Germanus makes the Alb represent Christ's divinity, and His transfiguration on Mount Tabor.[2] The priest says in putting it on, "Purify me, O Lord, and cleanse my heart, that being washed in the blood of the Lamb I may enjoy everlasting bliss."

THE GIRDLE.

The Girdle is a cord made of twisted linen thread, and serves to fasten the Alb decently and commodiously about the priest's body. It was used in all sacrifices in the old law, by God's command. The Israelites, in eating the paschal lamb, were to "gird their loins." In the mystical signification,

---

[1] Cat. Scrip.   [2] Matt. xvii.

EXPLANATION OF THE MASS. 17

Isaiah says of Christ in His spiritual kingdom,[1] "Justice shall be the girdle of his reins." Our Saviour bids us have our loins girt,[2] that is, to restrain our irregular passions and lusts. In the tying the girdle the priest says, "Gird me, O Lord, with the cincture of purity, and extinguish in my loins all incentives of concupiscence, that the virtue of continence and chastity may remain in me."

THE MANIPLE.

The Maniple, worn on the left arm, was formerly of linen. Ven. Bede derives its etymology from *mappa*, a towel, and it served as a handkerchief to wipe off the tears which devout celebrants were accustomed to shed during the sacred mysteries. The prayer in putting it on, which is, "Let me, O Lord, deserve to wear the maniple of weeping and sorrow, that with exultation, I may receive the reward of my labor," seems to refer to the 125th Psalm, "They who sow in tears shall reap in joy: Going they went and wept, casting their seeds, but coming they shall come with joyfulness carrying

---
[1] Isaiah xi.   [2] Luke xii.

their sheaves." Since the time of Pope Sylvester, in the fourth century, it has generally been of the same stuff as the stole and chasuble.

STOLE.

The word Stole signifies a robe, and, in Scripture, is often taken for a mark of dignity and power. So Pharaoh put on Joseph a silken stole.[1] The stole and ring, Plutarch says, were worn by magistrates and priests. "Moses put on Aaron a stole of glory."[2] In the parable of the Prodigal,[3] the father orders the stole and ring to be put on his penitent son as marks of restored honor; and the priest, in putting on this vestment, expresses well its signification, saying, "Restore unto me, O Lord, the stole of immortality, which I lost in the prevarication of our first parent; and although I come unworthily to thy sacred mystery, yet may I deserve everlasting joy." Acknowledging, like the true penitent, his unworthiness, yet placing a lively confidence in God.

The stole, with some alteration of form, has always been used in the Church as a suitable badge

---

[1] Gen. xli.   [2] Eccles. xlv.   [3] St. Luke xv.

EXPLANATION OF THE MASS. 19

of the dignity and quality of the priests in the new law.[1]

CHASUBLE.

The Chasuble, in Latin *Casula*, which signifies a small cottage, or a covering for the body, is the upper vestment, and is only worn by the celebrant during Mass. The Greeks wear it full round, hanging on all sides over the shoulders, almost to the ground, and clasped before. The Latins have it hanging down behind and before, but open on each side, or what the French call *enchancre*. It seems to refer to the hyacinthine ephod of the high priest in the law of Moses. It has also relation to the purple garment put upon our Saviour in derision by the soldiers. In putting on this badge of dignity, the priest says, "O Lord, who hast said my yoke is sweet and my burden light, enable me so bear it, that I may obtain thy grace. Amen." — In allusion to our blessed Saviour's kind invitation, Come to me all you that labor, etc.[2]

The vestments used in the Mass and Divine office are of different colors, on different festivals

---
[1] Origen, St. Basil, Rabanus, etc.   [2] Matt. xi. 28.

of the year; the colors adopted having a symbolical meaning. Thus white, emblematic of purity, is used on the festivals of Confessors, Holy Virgins, Festivals of the Blessed Virgin Mary, etc. Red, suggestive of blood, is used on the feast days of Martyrs, and festivals allusive to the Passion and Precious Blood of our Divine Lord, etc. Green, which is a kind of medium color between red, white, and black, on ferials and vigils. Purple, which is a kind of semi-mourning, on fast days, in Advent, Lent, etc.: and black, in Masses and offices for the dead. All other colors are forbidden.

THE ALTAR.

Sacrifice, Priest, and Altar, are correlatives, and must necessarily go together. The Latin *Ara* is derived from *Andere*, to burn, and *Altare* from *altus*, high, because it is an elevated structure to sacrifice upon. The erection and use of altars under the law of nature and the law of Moses are so often mentioned in history, sacred and profane, that it were superfluous to adduce proofs of them. The use of altars in the new law is denied by those sects who use none; yet they may be conscious of their existence and use before themselves, by the remaining ruins of those which they have destroyed and profaned.

The authority of the Altar or table used by our Blessed Saviour at the institution of the Eucharistic sacrifice and sacrament, and which was prefigured by the table of proposition joined with the texts of St. Paul,[1] "We have an altar, whereof they have no power to eat who serve the tabernacle," and, again, where he contrasts the table of the Lord with the table of devils.[2] These authorities, I say, and many others, are certainly sufficient. To these also we might add the testimonies of Fathers, Councils, and the uninterrupted practice of the Church.

CRUCIFIX AND CANDLES.

To Protestants we might apologize for the custom of having a crucifix and candles upon the altar, by the example of Queen Elizabeth, that great apostle of the Reformation and head of the Church of England, who kept upon her altar, in her private chapel, a crucifix and candles, though

---
[1] Heb. xiii. 10.   [2] I Cor. x. 24.

the candles were never lighted. But we have better authority and patterns to follow: St. Paul says:

"For the word of the Cross, to them indeed that perish, is foolishness; but to them that are saved, that is, to us, it is the power of God." [1]

"But we preach Christ crucified, unto the Jews, indeed, a stumbling-block, and unto the Gentiles foolishness." [2]

"God forbid that I should glory, save in the Cross of our Lord Jesus Christ." [3]

Our Saviour commands us to commemorate His passion and death in celebrating the Eucharist; and can it be a crime to place before our eyes what recalls in a lively manner Christ's dying on the cross.

In the four last books of the Pentateuch we find repeated prescriptions for lamps and lights to be kept in the temple, and particularly during the sacrifices. The Christians observed this from the earliest ages. We find them mentioned in the fourth of those canons attributed to the apostles. In the fourth age of the Church, one Vigilantius, a profligate priest, in the parish of Barcelona, set himself

---

[1] I Cor. I. 18.   [2] I Cor. I. 23.   [3] Gal. vi. 14.

up for a *wit*, like Voltaire and his disciples in modern times, to turn into ridicule many of the pious customs, ceremonies, and the discipline of the Church, and amongst others, the burning of tapers while the sun shone. He met with an over-match in his contemporary, St. Jerome, whose able and masterly pen made his adversary smart at every stroke. He tells him, Judas grudged the precious ointment which the woman poured on our Saviour's head, and *Vigilantius* (or rather Dormitantius, as he calls him, playing upon his name) seems to grudge what is equally intended to honor Christ. Our Redeemer needed not the ointment, yet He received it in good part, and commended the pious intentions of her who bestowed it. He needs not the lights placed on the altar; but approves of the pious dispositions of the faithful. Tapers are used when the sun shines, not to expel darkness, but to demonstrate our joy, as illuminations are used in public rejoicings. Light is an emblem of purity and of faith, as the oil is of charity or grace. The wise virgins in the Gospel[1] kept their lamps burning. Our Saviour[2] bids us have lamps burning in our

---

[1] St. Matt. xxv.   [2] Luke xii.

hands, and to be always ready at a call. St. John Baptist was a burning light.[1] Our Saviour himself was a "light for the revelation of the Gentiles and the glory of his people Israel."[2] The word of God is characterized under the metaphor of light:[3] "Thy word is lucid, enlightening the eyes. Thy word is a lamp to my feet, and a light to my paths."

BEGINNING OF THE MASS.

The priest, considering himself as the ambassador of God, and having his commission and authority from Christ Jesus, yet reflecting on his own unworthiness, descends to the foot of the altar, and, in the sentiments of the humble publican, begins the preparatory part of the Sacrifice by the sign of the Cross, and in the name of the Father, the Son, and of the Holy Ghost. The sign of the Cross is the sign of our salvation, the abridgment of our profession of faith. The Cross is the instrument of our redemption, and will be the "sign of the Son of Man,"[4] and His standard borne before Him when He comes to judge the world. It was unfurled on the banners of the imperial army

---

[1] John v.   [2] Luke i.   [3] Ps. cxviii. 10.   [4] Matt. xxiv. 30.

soon as the Emperor Constantine became Christian, and laid his sceptre and diadem at the feet of a crucified Saviour.

THE CONFITEOR OR CONFESSION.

The Confiteor, said alternately by the priest and the people, appears in all the Liturgies of the Church, and is believed to have been ordained by the apostles. The Sarum Missal, anciently used in England, has the following abridged form of it. "I confess to God, to the Blessed Virgin Mary, to all the saints, and to you, that I have very much sinned in thought, word, and deed, my fault: And I beseech holy Mary, and all the saints of God, and you, to pray for me."

To confess to God cannot certainly be found fault with; nor to one another; since St. James says, "Confess your sins to one another."[1] But why confess to angels and departed saints, and desire their prayers? How can they hear us? And if they did, does it not injure the office of Christ, who is called our only Mediator? Our Saviour tells us that the angels (and the same may

---

[2] James v.

be said of the saints) rejoice at the conversion of a sinner.[1] They must, therefore, know of that conversion; and our humble confession of our sins is a good sign of penitence and conversion. Spirits do not communicate and receive knowledge by voice and ears, but by spiritual vision. Why may they not know our thoughts directed to them, as they do those of each other? Our petitions may be made known to them by our guardian angels; or, finally, seeing God, they see all things in Him.

Our Saviour's mediation is no more injured by begging the prayers of the angels and saints, than by desiring the prayers of one another. The angels do pray for us.[2] "O Lord of hosts, how long wilt thou not have mercy on Jerusalem, with which thou hast been angry these seventy years?"— and the angel received a favorable answer.[3] "The smoke of the incense of the prayers of the saints ascended before God from the hand of the angel." The Greeks, in their Liturgy, say, "First honoring her, who, in incorrupted virginity, brought forth the Son, we implore her intercession for us, saying, O Saviour, keep us by the prayers of thy

---

[1] Luke x. 15.   [2] Zach. i. 12.   [3] Rev. viii. 4.

mother." In the Liturgy of St. James, it is said: "We make commemoration of the most immaculate, most glorious, and Blessed Lady, Mother of God, and ever Virgin Mary, and of all the saints and just, that, by their prayers and intercession, we may obtain mercy." A similar form is found in the Liturgy of St. Chrysostom.

The priest ascends again to the altar, saying, "Take away from us, we beseech thee, O Lord, our iniquities, that we may approach the Holy of Holies with pure minds." Then kissing the altar, with reverence and respect to Christ, he says: "We pray thee, O Lord, by the merits of the saints, whose relics are here, and of all the saints, that thou wouldst vouchsafe to forgive all my sins!"

RELICS.

The primitive Christians were accustomed to meet at the graves of the Martyrs, especially on the anniversaries of their martyrdom, and there offered the sacred mysteries on their tombs. Afterwards, churches were built on those spots, or their remains were translated and deposited under the altar. So did St. Ambrose in regard to the relics of Saints Gervase and Protase.[1]

The Seventh General Council, held at Nice, 787, decrees, that if any churches had been consecrated without the relics of Martyrs, some relics should be deposited in them. Finally, all Church histories, Councils, and Fathers agree, that both Greeks and Latins were accustomed to place relics under the altar.

St. Cyril, of Jerusalem, and Patriarch of that See, in the year 350, remarks, that not only the souls of Saints are to be honored, but God has been also pleased to honor their bodies by great miracles. He mentions the examples of a dead man raised to life by the touch of the dead body of Elisha.[2] Also, the handkerchiefs and aprons which had touched the body of St. Paul.[3] We may add to these the miracles wrought by the shadow of St. Peter,[4] and by the mantle of Elias or Elijah.[5]

Naaman, the Syrian, sought leave of Elisha to carry away two mules' burden of earth from Judea[6] (which he considered as sanctified), in order to sacrifice to God thereon.

---

[1] Life of St. Ambrose. [2] IV Kings xiii. 21. [3] Acts xix. 12.
[4] Acts v. 15. [5] IV Kings ii. 14. [6] IV Kings v. 17.

St. Jerome, against Vigilantius, profusely and victoriously shows the practice of the Church in this regard, and confutes those who rashly found fault with it.

CHAPTER III.

INTROIT.[1]

THE priest goes to the book, and reads the Introït, or entrance upon the Mass. He signs himself again with the sign of the Cross, to make profession of his faith, and arm himself in virtue of Christ's passion. The Introït is a short sentence, generally from the Psalms, and suited to the office of the day, with the " Glory be to the Father," etc.

The primitive Church used here longer Psalms and prayers. St. Chrysostom, St. Basil, and others, shortened them to avoid prolixity, and suit the office to the declining devotion of the people.

The Κυριε Ελεησον (*Kyrie Eleison*), " Lord have mercy on us," was used from the highest antiquity. It is a most devout prayer, and is frequently found in Scripture, especially in the Psalms. For its frequent repetition, we have a good precedent in our Saviour's prayer in the Garden of Olives. It is recited in Greek, as having a peculiar energy in that language. So we retain many other words

---

[1] A Latin word, meaning " He enters, or goes in."

from the Greek, which cannot be so aptly expressed in our language, such as Bible, Epistle, Canon, Baptism, Eucharist, Christ, Angel, Prophet, Patriarch, Apostle, Martyr, etc. It is also to show that the Greeks and Latins make but one Church.

THE GLORIA.

The GLORIA IN EXCELSIS is called the Angelical Hymn, because it was sung at our Saviour's natal hour by the celestial choir. The angel who addressed the shepherds assigns the reason: "Behold I announce to you great joy; because this day is born to you a Saviour, who is Christ our Lord." "And suddenly there was with the angel a multitude of the heavenly host, praising God, and saying, Glory to God in the highest, and on earth peace to men of good will," or, as it is in the Greek, "on earth peace and good will among men." It seems to have been used from the apostles' time. St. Clement mentions it in the Apostolic Constitutions. Pope Telesphorus, in the year 142, enjoins it to be sung at midnight on the feast of Christ's Nativity. It is probable that some additions have been made by the early

Fathers. We have many pious hymns from St. Hilary, St. Ambrose, etc.

DOMINUS VOBISCUM.

The priest, during the sacrifice, turns several times to the people and greets them with this pious benediction, "The Lord be with you;" and the people answer, "And with thy spirit,"—to show the unity of priest and people. We find such turnings and salutations in the most ancient Liturgies. They refer to our Blessed Saviour's going thrice to address His disciples in the garden of Gethsemane. Once He turned to Peter with a look of mercy, to convert him, after he had denied his heavenly Master; and, finally, He turned towards the holy women (who followed Him weeping to the Calvary), and with a tender and salutary admonition: "Ye daughters of Jerusalem, weep not for me," etc. In some churches, the priest stands with his face to the people, and therefore does not turn round.[1]

---

[1] In these churches, such as the Basilicas in Rome, the altar is detached from the wall and the front is towards the apse of the church, the back of the altar being towards the people.

THE COLLECTS OR PRAYERS.

The prayer of the Sunday or Festival, together with the Epistle and Gospel, being every day different, is read in the vernacular language, and generally explained, or some instructive or pious discourse made from them. The Apostle admonishes that "Prayers, supplications, and thanksgivings should be made for all men," etc.[1] The Fathers particularly apply these words to the public Liturgy. In these prayers, supplications are made for the necessities of the people, or for a deliverance from evils; for benefits, graces, and favors, both general and particular; for the conversion of sinners; as also, to give thanks for mercies and bounties received.

They are called Collects from all these intentions together, and because they are made for and over all the faithful collected, and united with each other, and with the priest officiating.

THE EPISTLE,

as well as the Gospel, is found in the most ancient Liturgies; though it is generally believed

---
[1] I Tim. ii.

that the present Epistles and Gospels read at Mass were extracted from the Old and New Testaments, and disposed in order for the whole year, by St. Jerome, at the command of Pope Damasus. They are called Epistles, because they are often taken from the Epistles of St. Paul, or those of the other apostles. As also, because they are, as it were, a missive letter addressed to us by God through the pens of the prophets and apostles, to dispose us for the reception of His Gospel. The Epistle precedes the Gospel as the law and the prophets went before grace, the preaching of St. John the Baptist before that of our Blessed Saviour.

At the end of the Epistle, the faithful were wont to say *Pax tecum*, " Peace be with thee ; " they now say *Deo gratias*, following the example of St. Paul,[1] "Thanks to God for his unspeakable gift ; " viz., in sending the prophets and apostles to teach us the way of salvation. Nothing, says St. Augustine, "can more briefly or usefully express the grateful effusion of our heart than *Deo Gratias.*"

[1] II Cor. ix.

THE GRADUAL

is a versicle or responsory to the Epistle, suited to the joy or sorrow expressed therein. It is called *gradual*, because some of the choristers ascend the *steps* of the choir to begin it. In times of joy, Alleluia, or Hallelujah, is said or repeated; and this word, which is an ejaculation of praise and joy, is retained in the Hebrew language amongst Greeks, Latins, and all nations, as not having any word that can so well or so forcibly express its signification.

THE GOSPEL

is an extract from one or other of the four Evangelists. It is called in Greek $\epsilon\nu\alpha\gamma\gamma\epsilon\lambda\iota o\nu$, Evangel, or happy message; in our language, Gospel, *i.e.*, God's spell, or letter, or word sent to us.

We find from St. Denis' "Ecclesiastical Hierarchy," and from the most ancient Fathers and Councils, that the Gospel was always read or sung before the Offertory, and the bishop or priest officiating, generally, gave some exposition, tract, or homily thereon.

This is the most excellent portion of the Scriptures. In other books of the Holy Scripture, the Holy Ghost opened the mouths and directed the pens of their writers; but in the Gospel, God opened His own mouth and taught us. We ought, therefore, to read or hear the Gospel with the same reverence as if we heard Christ Himself delivering it; and, hence, the faithful all stand up while it is read in Mass. Before the Gospel, the book is removed from the right to the left corner of the altar, to signify that the Gospel was preached to the Gentiles when the Jews unhappily rejected it. Meantime, the priest, reverently bowing before the middle of the altar, prays thus: "Cleanse my heart and my lips, Almighty God; and as thou didst, with a fiery coal, cleanse the lips of the prophet Isaiah, so vouchsafe to cleanse me by thy gracious mercy, that I may worthily announce thy Holy Gospel, through Christ our Lord. Amen."

Then humbly imploring the divine leave and benediction, he says, "Our Lord be in my heart and on my lips, that I may worthily and competently announce his Gospel," — he then mentions the name of the Evangelist from whom the Gospel of the day is taken, and signs the book, and his own forehead, and lips, and breast, to show he *is not ashamed of the Gospel of Christ*. The people, with joyful acclaim, say, " Glory be unto thee, O Lord." At the end of the Gospel he kisses the book in reverence to God's word, and begs that, by virtue of the evangelical doctrine, our sins may be blotted out; and the people, signing themselves, devoutly reply, "Praise to thee, O Christ."

THE CREED.

The Apostles' Creed was said for the first three hundred years; but afterwards, in condemnation of the Arian impiety, the Fathers of the Council of Nice more fully extended this symbol of our faith, to express our sincere belief of the divinity of Christ and His consubstantiality with the Father. The first Council of Constantinople, in opposition to Macedonius, added, that the Holy Ghost proceeds from the Father and the Son. The people stand during its recital, to show their promptitude and readiness to put in execution what is propounded in the Creed. They kneel at the words

"*Et homo factus est*" ("and was made man"),[1] humbly to adore Him whom God the Father commanded the angels to adore.

Here ends what is called the Mass of the Catechumens, because then those who were not baptized were accustomed to retire.

THE OFFERTORY.

The Offertory begins by a sentence or verse so named, commonly taken from the Psalms, and corresponding to the Introït, but varying according to the times or festivals. It is also of the earliest antiquity, and formerly consisted of longer canticles or hymns during the time that the faithful made their offerings, as they were accustomed to do for the matter of the sacrifice, as also for maintenance of the clergy, and for the relief of the poor. Mystically it represents our Saviour's admonition to His apostles in the garden, and the oblation He there made of Himself to His Almighty Father, accepting of the bitter chalice of His passion.

The priest, in taking the veil off the chalice, represents the unveiling of the old law, whose

---

[1] Heb. 1.

figures and types gave way to the substance of which they were shadows; and here, properly speaking, begin the functions of the priesthood, by making a solemn oblation of the matter of the sacrifice in reference to what it is to become.

Offering the bread on the paten, he says, "Receive, O Holy Father Almighty and everlasting God, this immaculate Host, which I, thy unworthy servant, offer thee, my living and true God, for my innumerable sins, offences, and negligences, and for all who are here present, and also for all faithful Christians living and dead, that it may avail both me and them to everlasting life. Amen."

He then puts some wine into the chalice, mingling with it a little water. This mixture is also venerable for its antiquity. St. Cyprian and St. Cyril defend the practice, and condemn its opposers. It represents the blood and water which issued from our Saviour's side; the union of our soul and body; the union of the two natures in Christ; and, finally, the union of Jesus Christ with His Church. The water represents the faithful, and is blessed; the wine represents Christ Himself, who needs no benediction. The prayer said, in pouring the water into the wine, is, "O God, who, in creating human nature, hast wonderfully dignified it, and reformed it again by a yet greater miracle, grant that, by the mystery of this water and wine, we may be made partakers of his divinity, who vouchsafed to become partakers of our humanity; namely, Jesus Christ, thy Son, our Lord, who with thee, in the unity of the Holy Ghost, liveth and reigneth one God, world without end. Amen."

Offering the chalice, he prays as follows: "We offer thee, O Lord, the chalice of salvation, beseeching thy clemency that it may ascend before thy divine Majesty as a most sweet odor, for our salvation and that of the whole world. Amen." Then bowing down, he says, "Accept us, O Lord, in the spirit of humility and a contrite heart, and grant that the sacrifice we offer this day may be pleasing to thee, O Lord God."

Blessing the bread and wine, he says, "Come, Almighty God the sanctifier, and bless ✠ this sacrifice prepared for the glory of thy holy name."

He then washes the tips of his fingers at the corner of the altar, that nothing may adhere to the

EXPLANATION OF THE MASS.

thumbs and forefingers which are to touch the blessed Sacrament, and to signify the sanctity, purity, and innocence of soul necessary for offering and receiving the sacred mysteries; to implore which, he recites, in the meantime, as is found in the Liturgy of St. Peter, part of the 25th, *alias*, 26th Psalm, "I will wash my hands among the innocent, and will compass thy altar, O Lord," etc. Then returning to the middle of the altar with fervent devotion, he lays his hands on the altar, and finishes the oblation with this prayer: "Receive, O holy Trinity, this oblation which we offer thee in memory of the passion, resurrection, and ascension of our Lord Jesus Christ, and in honor of blessed Mary ever Virgin, and of blessed John Baptist, and of the holy apostles Peter and Paul, of these and of all the saints, that it may be available to their honor and our salvation, and may they vouchsafe to intercede for us in heaven, whose memory we celebrate here on earth, through the same Christ our Lord. Amen."

ORATE FRATRES.

The priest having implored the intercession of

the saints, yet diffident of himself, and conscious that he is surrounded with infirmity, and knowing that the prayers of many are more powerful than any single prayer, and that, as St. Jerome says, "it is impossible that the prayers of many should not be heard," invites his brethren to join with him from mutual charity and interest, saying, "Brethren, pray that my sacrifice and yours may be acceptable with God the Father Almighty." And the faithful answer, "May our Lord receive this sacrifice from thy hands, to the glory and praise of his holy name, to our profit, and the good of all his Church." The priest replies "Amen."

THE SECRET PRAYER.

Having invited the people to pray, he leaves them in that happy employment, whilst he, with Anna, the mother of Samuel, speaks to God in heart,[1] and only moves his lips, whilst his voice is not heard at all; or, as holy Judith prays in tears of compunction, moving her lips in silence.[2] Such secret prayers are to be seen in all Liturgies.

---

[1] I Sam. 1.   [2] Judith xii. 6.

THE PREFACE.

The priest and people having prepared their hearts in silence, proceed to the holy action contained in the Canon, and in excess of spirit break forth with raised voices in the Prolustion or Preface to the principal part of the Mass, joining the angels in singing the divine praises. This Preface admits of some variety, according to the different seasons or festivals, and concludes with what the Greeks call the "Trisagion, or Holy, holy, holy, Lord God of Hosts, all the earth is full of thy glory,"[1] which Isaiah and St. John the Apostle heard the blessed spirits incessantly singing;[2] adding the hymn by which the children and pious crowd welcomed our Saviour into Jesusalem, "*Hosanna in the highest: Blessed is he who cometh in the name of our Lord: Hosanna in the highest,*"— entering into the simplicity and innocent dispositions of children, best suited to these adorable mysteries. "Have you never heard," said our Lord, "that out of the mouths of infants and sucklings thou hast perfected praise?"[3] This Pref-

---

[1] Isaiah vi.   [2] Apoc. iv.
[3] St. Matt. xxi. 16.

ace, as to the substance, accords with the most ancient Liturgies. The Church, united with angels, uses their words, and imitates those blessed spirits in giving all glory to the Lord God of Hosts. The hymn by which our Saviour was welcomed was an exclamation of holy exultation and joy, heard and approved of by our divine Redeemer; and the faithful have no less cause to praise and bless Him, who, by His infinite power, came into the world to redeem us by His passion; and who out of His infinite love is coming to us in this holy sacrifice, and to feed our souls in this blessed Sacrament. Shall not we, with all submission and reverence, expect and attend the invisible coming of our Lord, casting our vestments, that is, prostrating our bodies, before Him, and carrying the boughs of interior devotion and piety, that in true faith, lively hope, inflamed charity, and tranquillity of spirit, we may be prepared to meet our God the Lord of the Universe, in the honorable company of angels, and raising our hearts above all earthly things, enjoy abundance of spiritual delights? "Truly this is no other than the house of God and the gate of heaven."[1]

---

[1] Gen. xxviii. 17.

CHAPTER IV.

THE CANON.

CANON is a Greek word, which means "rule, measure, order:" it here signifies a standing ordinance of prayer. The precepts laid down in the Councils of the Church are called Canons; and certain benefices which subject those who enjoy them to the observance of stated rules in the hours of the divine office, are called Canonries or Canonicates. A few variations of this order of prayer, in certain solemnities, are prescribed; but the officient cannot alter them at his pleasure. Some difference of words, too, in this Canon, is found amongst ancient Liturgies, but the sense is nearly the same in all.

It is, and always was, said in solemn silence, and the faithful accompany the priest in silent prayer, knowing well what is doing, and the devotion proper for themselves during the time.

The priest, with heart and hands lifted up, supplicates the most clement Father, that through Jesus Christ His Son, our Lord, He would accept of and bless the matter prepared for the august Sacrifice, which elements he calls holy and unspotted, in reference to what they are soon to become.

PRAYER FOR THE CHURCH.

He prays, first, for the pacification, protection, union, and direction of the Holy Catholic Church of Christ, that she may be preserved and protected from all her enemies, united in her members, and guided in all truth by the superintendence and counsel of the Holy Spirit. She is the household of God and of faith; the spouse of Jesus Christ; and those separated from her are under a lamentable but just sentence of divorce.

FOR THE CHIEF BISHOP.

He prays for our Chief Bishop, who fills the chair of St. Peter, who is the Vicar of Jesus Christ, the visible Head of the Church, and the Centre of Unity; that he may be sanctified and assisted in the care and government of his numerous flock, and in his vigilance to perceive and to give the alarm when the insidious wolf approaches the fold. We have an early example of this pious duty,[1]

---

[1] Acts xii.

when St. Peter, being cast into prison, made the faithful dread, lest, the pastor being struck, the flock might be dispersed, and prayer was made without ceasing by the Church to God for him, etc.

THE ORDINARY OF THE PLACE.[1]

In all these prayers it is naturally understood that the faithful fervently join. As the Pope is not the only pastor, but each part of the mystical body has its particular guides and sentinels, we pray for the bishop to whose immediate care we are intrusted.

MEMENTO FOR THE LIVING.

We offer up our prayers for those who are recommended to us in particular, and for all those in whom, whether from duty or inclination, we are more particularly interested. We especially pray for one another, saying, "And of all here present whose faith and devotion is known unto thee, for whom we offer, or who offer up to thee, this sacrifice of praise, for themselves and for all theirs, for the redemption of their souls, for the hope of

---

[1] *i.e.*, the bishop.

their salvation and health, and who pay their vows to thee the eternal living and true God." To recall still the memory of Christ's passion, the word *memento* puts us in mind of the penitent thief's petition. Holy David also says, "Remember, O Lord, thy commiserations and mercies which are from the beginning."[1]

THE COMMUNICANTES.

The priest and people having now prayed for the pastors of God's Church, for each other, for all the members of the Church militant; for all that tends to increase faith, piety, and the peace and happiness of society; and even for all that are out of the pale of the Church, that they may happily be brought into her fold, — they extend also the communion of saints to the Church triumphant; and first of all, with all antiquity, commemorate the ever-glorious Virgin Mary, mother of our Lord Jesus Christ, in whose chaste womb was formed the Victim we are about to offer, from whose substance He received the sacred blood which flowed on the cross for our redemption, and which still

---

[1] Ps. xxiv.

mystically flows on our altars; the glorious apostles, too, whose privilege it was to learn from the mouth of Jesus Christ the value of this sacrifice, who received power from Him to offer it, and who actually offered it before us; as also the blessed martyrs, whose blood, mingled with that of the immaculate Lamb, was received as an agreeable holocaust. Finally, we add, — and of all the saints, *by whose merits and prayers* grant we may in all things be defended by the help of thy protection, through the same Christ our Lord. Amen.

How unjustly are we here accused of exalting the saints into Deities, and assimilating them to the Divinity itself! "Since we only beg the members of Jesus Christ, who are also our fellow members; His children, who are our brethren; His saints, who are also our first fruits, — to pray for us, and with us, to our common Master through our common Mediator. We acknowledge, in the greatest of the saints, no excellence but what flows from God; no merit or consideration before His eyes but from their virtue; no virtue but from His grace; no knowledge of human things but what He is pleased to communicate to them; no power to assist us by their prayers; no felicity but by perfect submission and conformity with His holy will."

HANC IGITUR OBLATIONEM.

"We, therefore, beseech thee, O Lord, graciously to accept this oblation of our servitude, as also of thy whole family, and dispose our days in thy peace, and preserve us from eternal damnation, and rank us in the number of thy elect, through Christ our Lord. Amen."

This prayer, in substance, is found in the ancient Liturgies. All, however, agree that St. Gregory the Great [1] added the three last pious petitions, for the peace of Christians, conversion of souls, of security from eternal misery, and that we may be ranked in the number of the elect. In saying this prayer, the priest spreads his hands over the bread and wine, which ceremony has always been used. It was prescribed to the priests of the Mosaic law,[2] that, in the oblation of the victim, he shall put his hands upon the head of the victim, and it shall be acceptable and help to his expiation, thereby, as it were, transferring his own guilt and

---
[1] Elected Pope A.D. 590.   [2] Lev. 1. 4.

that of the persons for whom the offering was made, upon the victim which was substituted in their place. Those sacrifices of the old law were but figures of the sacrifice which Christ offered for our sins, and which is represented in the Mass. Wherefore, the priest fitly lays his hands on what is to be offered, in a manner imposing his own sins, and those of the persons for whom he has made the *memento*, on Him who willingly bore them, that by His death He might expiate them and deliver us from eternal death. This ceremony, also, mystically represents the violence offered to our Saviour in the whole course of His passion, and, especially, the violent and racking extension of His blessed body upon the cross, by barbarians and hardhearted executioners, etc. Here our devotion will naturally suggest compassion for the sufferings of our Jesus. But let us be aware of renewing those torments,—of losing the benefit of this balm of peace, and rousing God's indignation by fresh outrages.

QUAM OBLATIONEM.

" Which oblation do thou, O Lord, vouchsafe, we beseech thee in all things to make ✠ blessed, ✠

approved, ✠ ratified, reasonable, and acceptable, that it may be made to us the ✠ body and ✠ blood of thy most beloved Son, our Lord Jesus Christ." This is the preparatory prayer and benediction immediately preceding the consecration, expressive of the priest's intention and the Church's belief, — imploring that the oblation may be *blessed* by the Holy Ghost; *approved* by the Deity, that thereby we may be enrolled in heaven; *ratified* in its effects, that we may be deemed the true members of His Church; *reasonable* in our faith; and that we may be acceptable to God in His Son. The sign of the cross is made thrice upon both kinds,[1] and then singly upon each. The words principally belong to the consecration of the Eucharist; the signs or ceremonies chiefly appertain to the remembrance of Christ's passion.

Here we are reminded of the emphatic expression by which the Almighty called light into existence: "Let there be light, and there was light." Here the Church says: May it be made the body and blood of Christ, and at her command the well beloved Son of the Father is ready to descend upon the altar under the Sacramental Elements.

---

[1] *i.e.*, over the bread or host, and over the wine in the chalice.

CONSECRATION.

We are now come to that miraculous action in which the holy sacrifice principally consists. The words are known to all Christians. They were spoken by Him who has the words of eternal life. The Catholic Church, finding nothing in the words which Jesus Christ made use of in the institution of this adorable mystery (Real Presence) that obliges us to understand them in a figurative sense, deems this sufficient reason for believing them in their plain, proper, and literal meaning, without being anxious or troubled *how* He effects what He says. We adhere precisely to His words. He who does what He pleases, in speaking effects what He says; and it is easier for the Son of God to force the laws of nature, in order to verify His words, than it is for us to accommodate our minds to violent interpretations which overthrow all the laws of speech.

Our Divine Redeemer, eagerly desirous to give us an ineffable pledge of His love, wishing to exercise our faith, and at the same time to obviate the natural horror of eating His flesh and drinking His blood in their proper form, in His wisdom

EXPLANATION OF THE MASS.

willed to give us them shrouded under another species. The repeated and clear promises previously made;[1] the words of the Institution, together with the circumstances attending that Institution; and the unanimous belief of all ages in all countries, testified by the writings of the Fathers, decrees of Councils, ecclesiastical histories, and the living voice of the greater part of Christians, even of schismatics for many centuries separated from the Church, — render us secure and quiet in our belief.

It belongs to those who have recourse to a figurative sense, and who have deviated into by-paths, to assign their reasons for their new-modelled doctrine, unknown to former ages; " 'Tis ours to captivate our understanding to the obedience of Christ,"[2] nor to dare to limit Almighty power to the narrow capacity of our reason, still less to confine it to the rule of our senses.

The priest performs this act of consecration in the person of Christ, relating His actions, conforming to His ceremonies at His Last Supper, and applying Christ's own words as the form which our Saviour Himself has left to His Church.

---

[1] St. John vi.   [2] II Cor. x. 5.

EXPLANATION OF THE MASS. 55

After each separate consecration, the priest first kneels down before the blessed Sacrament, in humble and fervent adoration; then elevates successively the Host and chalice, that the prostrate faithful may pay their adoration to their Saviour in this mystery of His love. The priests in the Mosaic law were commanded to "elevate the victims before the Lord."[1] The elevation of the Eucharist is mentioned in the most ancient Liturgies, and the learned St. Basil reckons it amongst the apostolical traditions.[2] Mystically, the elevation puts us in mind of our blessed Saviour's being raised up upon the cross; and causes us, in the deepest sentiments of contrition, gratitude, and awe, to adore that body which was broken for us, and that blood which was shed for the remission of our sins. By the twofold consecration, "This is my body, this is my blood," the body and blood of Christ are mystically separated, as they were really separated upon the cross; and this mystical separation contains a lively and efficacious representation of the violent death which He suffered. Thus the Son of God is placed upon the altar in

---

[1] Lev. ix. 21.   [2] Lib. de Spiritu Sancto.

virtue of these words, clothed with the signs which represent His death.

ENDS OF THE SACRIFICE.

This religious action carries along with it an acknowledgment of God's sovereignty; because Jesus Christ, truly present, renews and perpetuates the memory of His obedience, even unto the death of the Cross.

We present to the eternal Father our Eucharist, Christ Himself, and the infinite merit of His death, protesting that we have nothing else worthy of being offered Him in return for all His goodness.

We believe that the presence of Christ, our sole propitiatory victim, by His blood, causes the Father to look down propitiously on us.

We believe, also, that the presence of our Mediator is itself a most powerful intercession for mankind, especially, as the Apostle says,[1] that "in heaven itself he now appears in the presence of God for us."

Finally, we consecrate all our prayers by this divine offering; and we offer, at the same time, to

---
[1] Heb. ix.

EXPLANATION OF THE MASS.

the eternal Father, ourselves, in, with, and by His beloved Son, as living victims to His divine Majesty.

All this is performed in the prayers immediately following the Consecration, in which the death, resurrection, and ascension of our Lord are commemorated; offering to God a pure, holy, and immaculate host, the holy Bread of eternal life and the chalice of salvation, begging of God to accept of this unspotted Victim, as He was pleased to accept of the gifts of Abel, Abraham, and Melchisedec; and that as an angel was present at the sacrifice of Abraham,[1] so His angel may carry up before His throne the open hearts and fervent vows of those who assist at this sacrifice.

MEMENTO FOR THE FAITHFUL DEPARTED.

We extend the Communion of Saints to the Church suffering in a middle state, viz., those who are gone before us "with the sign of faith, and who sleep in the sleep of peace;"— naming those we particularly mean to pray for.

A Protestant author,[2] in a book printed in London, 1714, and which is entitled, "The Unbloody

---

[1] Gen. xxii. [2] John Johnson, M.A.

Sacrifice and Altar Unveiled and Supported," will save me the trouble of bringing proofs and documents for this faith and devotion. "There is one proof," says he, "of the propitiatory nature of the Eucharist, according to the sentiments of the ancient Church, which will be thought too great, and that is, the devotions used in the Liturgies, and so often spoken of by the Fathers, in behalf of deceased souls. There is, I suppose, no Liturgy without them, and the Fathers frequently speak of them. St. Chrysostom mentions it as an institution of the Apostles. St. Austin asserts that such prayers are beneficial to those who have led lives so moderately good as to deserve them. Cyril, of Jerusalem, mentions a prayer for those who are gone to sleep before us. Tertullian speaks of this practice as prevailing in his time. And the Constitutions do require priests and people to use those sorts of devotions for the souls of those who die in the faith." And adds:[1] "They judged it, therefore, lawful; and if it were lawful, no more need be said. Nature will do the rest."

It is distressing to observe this learned and

---

[1] pp. 287, 288.

painstaking author stumble for want of the true support and guide; for he confounds the commemoration made of the Blessed Virgin and other saints, with the prayers offered up for the faithful departed; and says, in the same place, "They prayed for the Virgin Mary, the apostles, patriarchs, and such as they believed to be like them." I need not here repeat what I have elsewhere inculcated to stimulate your devotion and charity to the performance of a duty to which nature and piety will jointly impel you. You have here a happy opportunity of exercising your charity and proving your genuine friendship; and those suffering souls borrow the words of the Scripture and the voice of the Church to solicit our aid: "At least you, my friends, have pity on me, for the hand of the Lord hath touched me."[1]

NOBIS QUOQUE PECCATORIBUS.

Returning, again, upon ourselves, we beat our breasts, acknowledging ourselves miserable sinners, yet hoping in the multitude of God's mercies, we entreat Him to admit us one day into the blessed

---
[1] Job xx.

society of the saints, not weighing our merit, but granting us pardon, through Christ our Lord, "by whom all things were made, who is our Sanctification and Redemption;" and "as in Adam all die, so in Christ shall all be made alive; in whom we are blessed with all spiritual blessings: by whom, in whom, and with whom, to God the Father Almighty, in unity of the Holy Ghost, be all honor and glory forever and ever. Amen."[1]

---

[1] John I.; I Cor. v.; Eph. v.; I Cor. xv.; Eph. I.

CHAPTER V.

PATER NOSTER.

THE priest introduces this most holy prayer, taught us by our Lord Himself, by a preface, inviting the faithful to join him in disposing their souls for a real or spiritual participation of the blessed Sacrament, expressing humility, and intimating that we durst not call God our Father, unless Christ had commanded and ordained that we should do so, saying, "Instructed by thy wholesome precepts, and taught by thy divine Institution, we presume to say, Our Father," etc.

The Liturgy which bears the name of St. Peter hath this variation: "Instructed by the divine doctrine, and taught by salutary admonition, we dare to say," etc. In the Liturgy of St. Basil it runs thus: "Vouchsafe, O Lord, that with confidence, and without reprehension, I may be bold to invoke thee, O supercelestial God the Father, and say," etc.

No prayer can be more suitable to prepare us for the Holy Communion. "He who prays not as Christ has taught is not Christ's disciple, and the

Father does not easily hear the prayer which the Son hath not dictated."[1] "He who made us to live hath taught us to pray; whilst we speak to the Father by the prayer which the Son hath taught, we shall more easily be heard."[2] It is so short in words that the dullest may learn it; so comprehensive in its meaning, that St. Cyprian and Tertullian call it " a summary of the Gospel."

Some authors maintain, that before the apostles settled the form or Canon of the Mass, they used only the Consecration and the Lord's Prayer. It is said aloud, and the assistants say the last petition; but the priest says "Amen," as the Mediator between God and His people. He then redoubles the *libera nos*, "Deliver us, O Lord, from all evils, past, present, and to come," etc., making a kind of amplification upon the last petition, begging that the blessed Virgin, St. Peter, and St. Paul (St. Gregory added St. Andrew, to whom he had a particular devotion), and all the saints, may join in obtaining for us a deliverance from the great evil of sin, and in obtaining peace and unity with God, peace and tranquillity among men, and

---

[1] St. Chrysostom. [2] St. Cyprian.

peace and concord within ourselves, in these our days of tribulation and affliction; and that, in this security, we may worthily participate of the holy Eucharist, the solace of our earthly pilgrimage. The low voice in which this prayer is said may represent the silence of the holy women, who prepared their spices to anoint our blessed Saviour's body, but rested on the Sabbath day according to the commandment.[1]

The priest, meantime, uncovers the paten, and lays the purificatory aside, in reference to the linen clothes which were found apart in the monument at the resurrection of Christ. He kisses the paten (as asking of God peace of soul and body), and reverently places it under the sacred Host. He then uncovers the chalice, kneels, and taking up the Host, breaks it over the chalice, that if any particles should fall off, the chalice may receive them. The breaking of the Host serves for the more commodious receiving it, and imitates what our blessed Saviour did at His Last Supper, and which the Church in all ages has observed. This ceremony is often mentioned in the New Testament.

---

[1] St. Luke xxiii.

St. Paul says[1] that "the bread which we break, is it not the communion of the body of Jesus Christ?" The disciples at Emmaus knew Christ "in the breaking of bread,"[2] which many Fathers understand of the Eucharist. The disciples also *assembled to break bread.* Although it be still called *bread,* this does not contradict the *Real Presence* or the miraculous change: since our Saviour often calls Himself the *bread of life,*[3] the true bread which came down from heaven.[4] The species only are divided. Our Saviour's body is incapable of fracture, division, or hurt; "he cannot die nor suffer any more;" so the soul of man is not broken or separated, although the parts of the body be amputated or separated from each other. He then makes thrice the sign of the cross with a particle of the host over the chalice, saying, "May the peace of our Lord be always with you." The people answer, "And with thy spirit." Upon this mutual agreement in the peace of Christ Jesus, he lets the particle fall into the chalice, saying, "May this mixture and consecration of the body

---

[1] I Cor. x.
St. John vi.
[2] St. Luke xxiv. 51.
[4] Rom. vi. 9.

EXPLANATION OF THE MASS.

and blood of our Lord Jesus Christ be to us who receive it effectual to life everlasting. Amen." This mixture, which is only of the elements, or species, signifies that there is but one Sacrament under both species, and has always been observed in the Church as an apostolical tradition.

It is mentioned in all the Liturgies. In that of St. Chrysostom it is thus: The priest, taking the particle, puts it into the chalice, saying, "The plenitude of the Holy Ghost, now and for ever, and world without end. Amen."

THE PAX DOMINI.

At the *Pax Domini*, in the primitive ages, the faithful were wont to salute one another, in remembrance of the salutation of Christ to His disciples after His resurrection, when He repeatedly said, "Peace be to you." "Whence," says St. Cyril, of Alexandria, "there is a certain law delivered unto us by the Church; for in all holy congregations we often salute one another in this manner." These salutations have long been left off among the people; but the kiss of peace is still passed around among religious orders, canons, and wherever the

Mass is celebrated with a choir of clerics; yet we ought still to contemplate the resurrection and the good tidings, and offer of peace made by our Saviour to men of good will."

AGNUS DEI.

Having adored the blessed Sacrament, the priest, bowing and striking his breast, says twice, " Lamb of God, who takest away the sins of the world, have mercy on us ; " and the third time he says, " Grant us peace." This is to be found in ancient Liturgies; but it is commonly believed that Pope Sergius, in the sixth century, ordained that it should be said thrice. This appellation of Lamb was given to our Saviour by the prophets Isaiah [1] and Jeremy; [2] by St. John the Baptist,[3] when he pointed out the Messiah, saying, " Behold the Lamb of God; behold him who taketh away the sins of the world." The Son of God is often called the Lamb by St. John in Revelation. With the ancients in the Apocalypse, and with all faithful Christians, let us humbly adore the Lamb Christ Jesus, saying, " To him who sitteth on the throne,

---
[1] Isaiah llli.　　[2] Jer. xi.　　[3] St. John i. 29, 36.

and to the Lamb, be benediction, and honor, and glory, and power for ever and ever."[1]

"O Lamb of God, who diedst on the cross for us, to take away sins, have mercy upon us according to the multitude of thy mercies. O Lamb of God, model of meekness, patience, and innocence, be to us a pacific host, a peace-offering; and so dispose our souls, that in true peace of conscience we may approach to thy holy sacrament."

The officiant then bowing in a submissive manner, with his hands joined on the altar, says the three following prayers, by way of immediate preparations for receiving:

PRAYERS BEFORE RECEIVING.

"Lord Jesus Christ, who saidst to thy apostles, I leave peace to you, my peace I give to you, regard not my sins, but the faith of thy Church, and vouchsafe her that peace and unity which is agreeable to thy holy will, who livest and reignest God for ever and ever. Amen."

He begs this peace by the faith of the Church; that peace which was proclaimed at our Saviour's

---

[1] Apoc. v.

birth, and which he bequeathed as his parting legacy. He begs for the Church that unity, that purity from error, heresy, and schism, without which she cannot be the spouse of Christ. He begs that unity and peace may reign among the faithful, sweetness and truth in their conversation, justice in their actions, and charity in their hearts.

Second Prayer. — "O Lord Jesus Christ, Son of the living God, who, by the will of thy Father, the Holy Ghost coöperating, hast by thy death given life to the world, deliver me, by this most sacred body and blood, from all my iniquities, and from all evils, and make me always adhere to thy commandments, and never suffer me to be separated from thee, who livest and reignest God, world without end. Amen."

In this prayer he humbly begs a deliverance from sin, and all the evil consequences thereof; a constant fidelity in keeping God's commandments; and an inseparable union with the divine Saviour. "If, therefore," says St. Hilary, "Christ hath assumed the flesh of our body, and be truly the man who was born of Mary, we also do truly take the flesh of his body under the mystery; and by this we shall be one, because the Father is in him, and he in us."

THIRD PRAYER. — "Let not the participation of thy body, O Lord, turn to my judgment and condemnation; but let it through thy mercy be available to the safeguard and remedy both of the soul and body, who with God the Father, in the unity of the Holy Ghost, livest and reignest God for ever and ever. Amen."

"Let us labor as much as we can with God's help, that we may come with a pure and sincere conscience, and with a clean heart and chaste body, to the altar of our Lord, and deserve to receive the body and blood, not to judgment, but for the remedy of our soul."[1]

"Our body cannot obtain immortality, unless it be joined to the immortal body of Christ."[2]

The assistants, by understanding these prayers, and joining their intention and devotion with the priest may dispose themselves for a real participation of the sacred mysteries, or for a spiritual communion, of which a form will be subjoined.

---

[1] St. Augustine. [2] St. Greg. Nys.

THE COMMUNION.

The priest now proceeding to receive the blessed Sacrament, and consume the sacrifice, first kneels in adoration. "No one," says St. Austin, "eats this flesh of Christ without first adoring it." Taking the sacred Host into his hands, he says, " I will take the bread of heaven, and will call upon the name of the Lord." He thrice strikes his breast, saying, " Lord, I am not worthy that thou shouldest enter under my roof: say only the word, and my soul shall be healed. The body of our Lord Jesus Christ preserve my soul to everlasting life. Amen." Pausing a little, he kneels again, and says, " What shall I render to our Lord for all things that he hath given to me? I will take the chalice of salvation, and I will call upon the name of the Lord. I will call on our Lord in praising him, and I shall be safe from my enemies." Receiving the chalice, he says, " The blood of our Lord Jesus Christ preserve my soul to everlasting life. Amen." And here, if there be communicants, the Communion is administered with the words and ceremonies known to everybody. Nor need I here detain you by detailing the devotion of soul and reverence of body with which the communicant ought to approach to this sacred and life-giving banquet.

COMMUNION IN ONE KIND.

And here it may be proper to say a few words upon communion in one kind, so much found fault with by modern sectaries. From what has been already said, it is clear that Catholics have always held the Eucharist to be both a sacrifice and a Sacrament. As a sacrifice, they hold both kinds necessary, for the perfect representation of our Saviour's passion and offering him up to His eternal Father, under the appearance of death; but as a Sacrament only, they believe there is no precept of Christ for or against receiving in both kinds, and that communion in one or in both species is a matter of exterior discipline, left to the judgment and discretion of the Church, which, as the Council of Trent says,[1] always considered herself as possessed of the power, in the dispensation of the Sacraments (the substance or essence remaining entire), to enact or change what, according to the circumstances of time and place, she should judge

---

[1] Sess. 21, c. 2.

expedient for the advantage of the receivers, or the respect due to the Sacraments themselves. That St. Paul had pretty clearly pointed out this authority, saying, "So let a man deem us as the ministers of Christ, and the dispensers of the mysteries of God,"[1] and had availed himself of this license in correcting certain abuses in regard to the sacrament of the Eucharist, by his Epistle, and deferring other regulations for his personal arrival and observation: "And the rest I will set in order when I come."[2]

That, in the early ages of Christianity, the Sacrament had frequently been administered in both kinds; but that, in process of time, the custom being almost generally changed, the Church, conscious of her authority, and actuated by weighty and just reasons, had approved of communion in one kind, and enacted it as a law which, without the authority of the Church, it was forbidden to reject or to change.

These words of Christ are objected to us, "Except you eat the flesh of the Son of Man, and drink his blood, you shall not have life in you."[3]

---

[1] I Cor. iv. 2.   [2] I Cor. xi. 34.   [3] John vi. 54.

EXPLANATION OF THE MASS. 73

The greater part of Protestants deny these words to concern the Eucharist at all; and therefore they have an ill grace to object them to us.

In connection with this text we may cite St. Paul: "Therefore, whosoever shall eat this bread or drink this chalice of the Lord unworthily shall be guilty of the body and of the blood of the Lord" (I Cor. xi. 27). These words show clearly that St. Paul acknowledged that the reception of the Sacrament under either one or the other kind implied receiving both the *body* and *blood* of Christ. This text has been corrupted in the English (Protestant) versions of the Bible printed in 1562, 1577, and 1599, and reads as follows: "Eat this bread *and* drink," etc., instead of "or drink," in order to sanction communion under both kinds; but all the ancient codices and versions, both Greek and Latin, give the disjunctive conjunction "*or*" (Greek "ἢ πίνῃ," not "καὶ πίνῃ," Latin "*vel biberit*," not "*et biberit*"). The latest revised and "authorized version," however, of the English Testament of 1881 goes back to the original and correct sources, as in many other points, and gives the text correctly, "*or drink.*"

Admitting them, as we do, literally to regard the

holy Eucharist, we must confront this proposition with other propositions from the same chapter, *e.g.*, "This is the bread which cometh down from heaven, that if any man eat of it he may not die."[1] Here eating alone excludes death; and, again, "If any man eat of this bread, he shall live forever."[2] Here life is promised to eating alone. All these propositions flowed from the mouth of our Saviour. They cannot, then, be contradictory to each other; but they would necessarily be so if the first implied a precept of receiving both kinds. It therefore simply means that we must receive both body and blood; and, as every Catholic believes the Real Presence, he cannot doubt but, in receiving either species, he receives the true body and blood of our Saviour, there being now no separation of the one from the other.

But did not our Saviour, in giving the chalice to the apostles, say, *Drink ye all of this?*[3] He did so, and the same *all*, viz., the *apostles*, fulfilled the command; *and they all drank of it.*[4] This may imply a command to the bishops and priests who celebrate the holy mysteries to receive them under

[1] John vi. 50. [2] Ib. 52. [3] St. Matt. xxvi. 27. [4] St. Matt. xiv. 23.

both kinds, but not for the people in general, nor for the priests when they are not actually celebrating; and no bishop or priest not celebrating, not even on his death-bed, receives under both kinds.

These words, *Drink ye all of this*, can have no force against Catholics, unless it be proved that all the words which our Saviour addressed to the apostles at His Last Supper equally regarded all the faithful; now in that supposition, every lay man and woman would have the power to consecrate the Eucharist. This argument, therefore, by proving too much proves nothing.

The earliest Fathers and ecclesiastical historians make frequent mention of communion in one kind; as when in times of persecution the faithful were allowed to carry home the blessed Sacrament under the species of bread, and communicate themselves, to strengthen them in the trial they had to undergo. Sometimes even children were communicated, and that under the species of wine. Evagrius, Eusebius, St. Paulinus, Venerable Bede, etc., relate particular instances of communion in one kind only. Three general Councils approve and authorize it.[1]

---

[1] Constance, 1414; Basile, 1431; Trent, 1545.

Even the Acts of the Apostles insinuate it: The faithful were persevering in the doctrine of the apostles,[1] and in the communication of the breaking of bread, and in prayers.

The command for all the faithful to receive under both kinds, in order to discover the Manichæan heretics,[2] shows the practice of receiving, optionally, one or both kinds before that time.

That the Church is always ready to comply with every reasonable request, in point of discipline, when it can tend to promote the union of Christians, or bring back to the one sheepfold those who have by heresy gone astray, is manifested by the brief of Pope Pius IV.,[3] granting (at the earnest request of the Emperor Ferdinand) the use of the Chalice to certain states in Germany, upon certain conditions; but which producing little good effect, and rather increasing the insolence of farther demands, was revoked by succeeding Pontiffs.

FORM OF A SPIRITUAL COMMUNION.

Those who do not actually receive, ought at least to make a spiritual communion, of which the fol-

---
[1] Acts ii. 42.   [2] At Rome, 443, by St. Leo.   [3] Feb. 8, 1602.

EXPLANATION OF THE MASS. 77

lowing may serve as a form: "Throughout the offering of this holy sacrifice, O Lord, I have endeavored to fix the dissipation and inconsistency of my mind, and to meditate on thy passion and death here mystically renewed, and to beg of thee to apply its merits to my poor soul; yet I know that a participation of those mysteries of thy love is necessary to fulfil my duty as a joint offerer of this celestial victim, and to reap the full advantage of this sacred commemoration. I know it was thy intention in the institution, and that it is still the wish of thy Church, that all the faithful assistants should be prepared to communicate as well as the celebrant. It is my sincere desire to comply with thy gracious invitation, and the pious solicitude of thy spouse, our mother; but alas, O Lord! a just dread of my unworthiness, and the want of proper leisure to prepare for receiving thee into the habitation of my heart, deter me from approaching to thy holy altar; yet, divine Saviour, deign to cast a look of mercy on me at this distance, and impart to my soul, hungering after thee, at least the crumbs which fall from thy blessed and plentiful table. I am conscious I ought not to approach thee under the leprosy of sin; but I sincerely wish to be cleansed. I regret, from the inmost depths of my soul, all my disloyalties to thee, and here, with Magdalen, throw myself at thy feet, and wish to bathe them with penitential tears. O grant me the grace of a true contrition, and strengthen my resolutions of amending my life. Lord, I am not worthy that thou shouldest enter my roof; say only the word, and my miserable and languishing soul shall be healed. O Fountain of Mercy, suffer me at least to sigh after thee! I believe thou didst descend from the bosom of thy Father to take my nature, in order to redeem me from eternal misery. I believe thou wast the Priest and victim in the sacrifice of the Cross. I believe thy precious death loosed the sorrows of hell. I believe that thy glorious resurrection and triumphant ascension opened the gates of paradise. I believe the real presence of thy holy body and blood in these sacred mysteries; and I believe the worthily partaking of this divine Sacrament imparts spiritual life, and is a pledge of immortality. I believe; O Lord, help and quicken my languishing faith. My trust is in thee, who fillest the hungry with good things. Lord, my desire is before thee, and my sights are not hidden from thee. A contrite and humble heart thou wilt not despise. In thee, O Lord, I have hoped, let me never be confounded.

"Seduced by my corrupt desires, I unhappily deserted thy paternal guidance and thy plenteous mansion, that I might range through foreign climes in lawless liberty, and might loosen the reigns to my perverse inclinations. Alas! my happy portion of innocence and wholesome tuition was soon expended. I soon found, to my sad experience, that the land of indulgence and guilt is ever a region of misery; that I had exchanged the plenty of my Father's house for husks of swine.

"Behold me now returned, emaciated with hunger and covered with rags. Conscious of my ingratitude, degeneracy, and unworthiness to be ranked in the number of thy children, I beg thou wilt admit me as one of thy servants; for the meanest of thy domestics enjoyed a happy abundance, whilst I was perishing in want and misery. Yes, my dear Saviour, thou thyself art the food of my soul; may I feed on thee, be changed into thee, and become one spirit with thee. May these sacred mysteries communicate to me such effusion of thy charity, that I may embalm thy sacred body with the perfumes and sweet odor of every virtue, enwrap it in the fine linen of a pure conscience, and entomb it in a new and clean heart, that thou in me, and I in thee, may abide and repose for ever. Amen."

PRAYERS AT THE ABLUTION.

Taking the first ablution, the priest says, "Grant, O Lord, that what we have taken with our mouth, we may receive with a pure mind, and that, from a temporal gift, it may become to us an eternal remedy."

Taking the second ablution, he says, "May thy body, O Lord, which I have received, and thy blood which I have drunk, cleave to my bowels, and grant that no stain of sin remain in me, who have been nourished by thy pure and holy Sacraments, who livest and reignest for ever and ever. Amen." He then reads the versicle called the Communion, salutes the people, and bowing before the altar, says:

Final Prayer. — "Let the performance of my duty, O Holy Trinity, be pleasing to thee; and grant that the sacrifice which I unworthily have offered up to the sight of thy Majesty, may be acceptable to thee; and through thy mercy, be propitiatory to me and to all those for whom I have offered it, through Christ our Lord. Amen."

Final Blessing. — Then blessing the faithful, making the sign of the cross upon them, he says: "May the Almighty God, Father, Son, and Holy Ghost, bless you." ✠ And finishes by the beginning of the Gospel according to St. John, or such other Gospel as the office of the day may require.

Farewell, pious Reader! Mayst thou profit by the reading of this little treatise, and charitably pray for me.

INSTRUCTIONS BEFORE BAPTISM.

THE Sacrament of Baptism is an ordinance of our Lord Jesus Christ, by which we are delivered from the power of Satan, whose slaves we were born by sin, and, being washed by virtue of the Son of God, we receive a new birth; are made children of God by grace; incorporated in Christ; consecrated as temples of the Holy Ghost; and become living members of the Church, with an infallible right to eternal glory.

In this Sacrament, therefore, our souls are cleansed by the laver of water in the word of life.[1] This *water* and *word* are the *outward* mysterious *signs* of that *inward grace* by which the soul is here *cleansed* and sanctified, and are essential to Baptism. The other ceremonies, though not absolutely necessary, are, however, by no means to be omitted.

---

[1] Eph. v. 26.

INSTRUCTIONS BEFORE BAPTISM.

The person to be baptized is presented by his godfather and godmother, as his spiritual parents, and sureties for his baptismal engagements.

These give in his name; and having asked in it the *Faith*, and promised to keep the Commandments, different ceremonies are then performed to prepare the soul for the grace of Baptism; such as *blowing* thrice on the face in contempt of Satan, commanding him to "depart, and give place to the Holy Spirit:" the putting in the mouth a grain of *salt*, as an emblem of true *wisdom* and *discretion*, which seeks God in all things; and of the seasoning of the soul with the grace of Christ, to keep it from the corruption of sin: the repeated *exorcisms*, in order to cast out the devil: and the touching the ears with *spittle*, saying "Ephphatha! be thou opened," in imitation of Christ,[1] to signify the necessity of having the senses of the soul open to the truth and grace of God.

To a solemn renunciation of *Satan*, his *works* and *pomps*, succeeds the anointing on the breast with holy oil, to signify the unction of divine grace; be-

---
[1] Mark vii. 34.

tween the *shoulders*, to express the necessity of the same grace, to support the crosses we are to carry on our *shoulders* through the whole course of our lives.

Having professed the articles of our *Faith*, the Sacrament is administered by pouring *water* on the head, with the words ordained by Christ, viz., "I baptize thee in the name of the Father," etc.

The baptized person is afterward anointed on the top of the head, in the form of a *cross*, with the sacred *chrism*, and thereby consecrated in a particular manner to God; and cannot, without sacrilege, be profaned or alienated from His divine service. A white garment is then put on the head, to denote the robe of innocence, with which we are clothed in Baptism. And, lastly, a *burning taper* is put into the hand of the new Christian, to signify the *lamp* of faith which he, or she, is always to keep burning with the oil of charity, and good works, for the glory of God, the edification of neighbors; and with it be ever ready to go forth to meet the heavenly bridegroom, and to be admitted by him to that happy nuptial feast which knows no end.

Thus, dear reader, you see that the ceremonies used in Baptism are very expressive; and that they are by no means a subject of ridicule for the infidel, or unmeaning mummery to those unwise persons who have neither the time, the Scriptural knowledge, or, above all, the grace to investigate the deep and instructive nature of the Catholic offices in a spirit of prayer and unprejudiced search of truth.

INSTRUCTIONS BEFORE CHURCHING WOMEN.

I ANNOUNCE glad tidings to you. Your child is made a Christian, and the Catholic Church, the spouse of Jesus Christ, directs her minister to animate you to a fervent devotion in returning thanks for this great blessing. Beseech the Almighty to grant you length of life to rear your child in the holy faith in which it was baptized. It has been admitted into the Church militant, in the name of the Father, Son, and Holy Ghost. Take care to inculcate the divine virtues of faith, hope, and charity, by word and example, which will obtain for your child and yourself admission into the Church triumphant in heaven. Holding the candle in your hand is an emblem of your faith; and the 23d Psalm is read, that you may receive blessings from the Lord, and mercy from God your Saviour.

N B.— This Benediction is given only to such women as have brought forth in lawful wedlock.

INSTRUCTIONS BEFORE MATRIMONY.

THOSE who are to enter on the matrimonial state should know that Matrimony was originally instituted by God in the garden of Paradise. It was afterward ratified by the Son of God in the New Testament, honored with His first miracle, by changing water into wine at the nuptials of Cana in Galilee, and raised by Him to the dignity of a Sacrament, which confers upon the worthy receivers a sanctifying grace which will enable them to live together in a manner perfectly pleasing to God, and highly conducive to both their temporal and eternal welfare. St. Paul calls it a *Great Sacrament*, because the union that exists between the married pair is a mysterious representation of that union which exists between Christ and His Church, and also of that union which exists between His sacred Humanity and His Godhead.

Hence the importance of entering upon this holy state with the necessary dispositions, viz., a conscience free from mortal sin, by a good confession and worthy communion, lest by a profanation of this divine institution, instead of a blessing, you should entail on yourselves an endless train of miseries. Secondly, with purity of intention, to admit nothing which may be either incompatible with our spotless religion, or contrary to that modesty which becomes the Christian at all times, but more especially on so sacred and solemn an occasion. Thirdly, you must study to promote your mutual felicity, and concur together in all the concerns of life. Be careful to avoid those sharp contests and little disputes which, alas, embitter the marriage state and render it completely miserable. Bear with each other's weaknesses, that you may live in peace and harmony. But above all, never neglect the most essential duty in this state, viz., the religious education of your children, — if God should bless you with them. Teach them early the duties of a Christian life, as well by your example as your precept, that you and they, when time shall be no more, may enjoy eternal happiness.

RULES FOR ATTENDING AT MASS.

LOW MASS.

When the priest leaves the sacristy, the faithful rise and remain standing until the priest comes down from the altar to begin the first prayers. Then they all kneel, and remain so during the whole of the Mass, with the exception of the two Gospels. During the reading of the Gospels all stand. It is customary in some places to stand during the Creed. It is also allowed by custom to sit at the Offertory and after the Communion. The infirm are of course not bound to strict observance of these rules.

HIGH MASS.

The following are the rules to be observed at High Mass:

1. All rise when the priest leaves the sacristy, and remain standing until he comes down from the altar to say the first prayer.

2. Then all kneel until the priest intones the *Gloria*.

3. At the introduction of the *Gloria*, all rise, and remain standing until the priest sits down.

4. After the priest is seated the congregation sit down.

5. When the priest kisses the altar before the prayers, all rise and remain standing during the singing of the prayers.

6. When the Epistle is sung or read all sit down.

7. When the priest begins *Dominus Vobiscum*, before the Gospel, all rise and remain standing during the singing of the Gospel.

8. If the sermon follows the Gospel, the faithful kneel during the *Veni Creator*, stand at the reading of the Gospel, and sit down during the sermon. If the Bishop preaches, the faithful must remain standing, unless the Bishop invites them to sit down.

9. When the priest commences the *Credo* all rise. They kneel with the priest when he says *Et incarnatus est* (*i.e.*, And he was made flesh).

10. When the priest sits down the faithful also sit.

11. When the choir sings *Et incarnatus est* . . . *homo factus est*, the priest uncovers his head. *The faithful kneel.* Afterwards they sit down until the priest returns to the altar and kisses it.

12. Then all rise and stand during the *Dominus Vobiscum* and the *Oremus*.

13. Then all sit until the priest commences to say *Per omnia sæcula sæculorum*, before the Preface.

14. All rise at these words, and not at the *Sursum corda*.

15. All stand during the Preface.

16. From the Sanctus to the second Ablution after Communion all kneel.

17. At the second Ablution the faithful sit down until the priest kisses the altar to sing *Dominus Vobiscum* before the last prayers.

18. All stand during the last prayers, and remain so until the priest has sung *Ite missa est*.

19. All kneel then to receive the blessing.

20. During the last Gospel they all stand.

SOLEMN HIGH MASS.

At Solemn High Mass the same rules as for High Mass are applicable, with these two exceptions:

1. Whilst the celebrant reads the Gospel, the faithful remain sitting; they rise when the Deacon begins to sing the *Dominus Vobiscum*.

2. If the Censer-bearer incenses the congregation at the Offertory, all rise.

PONTIFICAL HIGH MASS.

The same rules for Solemn High Mass are applicable here also. If the Bishop preaches, the faithful must remain standing, unless the Bishop invites them to sit down.

CHOIR.

Concerning the choir the Rubric says: "Those who sing remain standing, but if they do not just now sing, all the rules above given apply to the choir." The Church allows the celebrant to sit down four times during the celebration of High Mass; viz., 1st, at the *Introït* and the *Kyrie ;* 2d, at the *Gloria ;* 3d, at the *Sequence*; and 4th, at the *Credo.* The choir is never allowed to omit even a single word in the piece. But all other pieces of music, *e.g.*, the *Sanctus*, the *Benedictus*, the *Agnus Dei*, must stop whenever the priest signifies his intention to proceed with the Mass. The *Sacrifice must not be interrupted by these pieces.* The Mass-server ought to give a sign with the bell before the Consecration; again when the priest is ready for the *Pater Noster*, and also before the last prayers. The choir should then stop singing.

MANNER OF ATTENDING AT VESPERS.

1. All should stand up when the celebrant is leaving the sacristy, and remain standing until he has arrived at the altar.

2. All should kneel whilst the celebrant is saying the first prayer at the foot of the altar; they rise when he rises to go to his seat, and remain standing until the celebrant sits down after intoning the *Deus in adjutorium*.

3. At the *Gloria Patri* at the end of each Psalm, all should bow the head, or stand up, where the custom exists.

4. During the singing of the *Chapter* at the end of the Psalms all should stand up, and remain standing until the celebrant is seated. If the celebrant should kneel during the singing of any hymn, the people should kneel also.

5. During the singing of the Anthem to the Blessed Virgin Mary, and during the *Magnificat* and prayer, the people should be standing.

6. When the celebrant kneels at the altar, before the exposition of the Blessed Sacrament, all should kneel, and remain so until the Blessed Sacrament is put into the tabernacle at the end of Benediction.

www.ingramcontent.com/pod-product-compliance
Lightning Source LLC
Chambersburg PA
CBHW020149170426

43199CB00010B/958